Survival Communication:

20 Ways to Ensure Communcation with Your Family During a Cataclysm

Table of content

Introduction

We've seen all sorts of disasters hit the world the past decade or so. The problem is that these kinds of disasters aren't just from Mother Nature, they are manmade and really could come at any time. The real question is are we prepared for whatever kind of catastrophe could come our way tomorrow or the next day?

Sometimes we think about things like shelter, food and water, but what happens if the people we care about most aren't all in the same place when that disaster strikes? Are we prepared with a plan to get reunited back together? Do we have the right equipment and the right training to ensure that we all unite again in a safe location?

It can be a scary and unsafe world in a matter of minutes if we don't have a plan, and we don't have the right equipment. However, if we are prepared and if our families and loved are prepared, we can sleep better every night knowing that we are ready for anything that might come tomorrow.

Chapter 1 – Things to Do First

With the world so unstable, we have to do a few things first to feel that sense of calm and preparedness. In order to get to the end, we have to start at the beginning. So here is where to start.

- **Create a Plan** – The most important part of any prepared individual is having a plan. Part of your plan should be a detailed list of every person you want to communicate with when disaster strikes. This should include a phone number, email address, full name, birth date, etc. It sounds a little scary to have all that information about them in one place, but it's important.

   Think about the fact that most of us don't memorize phone numbers anymore because they are just in ours cell phones for reference. In the event that your cell phone loses power, will you know all the phone numbers of the people you want to contact? Having phone numbers written down will give you the ability to contact everyone.

   You never know if and when you might need that information. You'll want copies of health insurance information for everyone in your family. If you leave town and end up needing a doctor or hospital care for whatever reason, you'll want to have that information with you.

The next part of creating your plan should include talking to everyone on the list. Who is the central contact person? Where is your meeting point and what is the first way you will try and contact everyone? If you can't use the first method, what is the back-up method? How long will you stay at the first meeting point? If it is unsafe, what is a back-up location? Think through all the details of your plan and talk through them with your group.

Making a plan that everyone knows is crucial for everyone to be a part of and included in the process. Even little ones can be part of the plan. They might be too young to be on their own, but that doesn't mean they can't understand what you are planning and what the broader picture is all about. It's important that everyone be included and everyone know what the entire plan is all about – the younger the better!

It may seem like a daunting task to explain why you are doing this, and you don't want to scare younger children, but unfortunately this is world we live in, and they shouldn't be sheltered from it. It should be explained – in the best manner possible – to them that you are being responsible and prepared, but that doesn't mean they should be scared. They should feel strong and prepared for whatever lies ahead. Only you, as the parent, know what is best for your child(ren), but including them in the plan is what we recommend, because if they are not home when disaster strikes, you'll want them to know how, when, and where to find you.

-   **Create a Code** – This doesn't need to be extremely complicated, but you'll want something that is unique to your group. You'll want something you can use if you post on social media or talk on the radios. That way you can talk about your group and where you are going without broadcasting to the rest of the world where you are going and what you are doing. However, your family and loved ones will know and be able to join you. It's partly for the safety of your group and partly for your privacy.

Ultimately it can just be code names for places and people, so if you are talking about your family and various locations others won't be able to follow you or locate you later.

Chapter 2 – Traditional and Non-Traditional Phones

Phones are probably the most obvious form of communication when it comes to a disaster. Some of them might be in service if you're lucky. Let's talk about the different ways you might be able to use a phone to communicate with your family.

- **Cell Phone** – Cell phones are basically attached to us at all times these days. If a disaster strikes, we always hope that they are working; however, we always have to plan that they won't be. The first thing to remember is that there may not be power, so if you know a disaster might be coming (i.e. a storm or natural disaster), charge up your phone and make sure you have a car charger so you have plenty of battery. Also, don't waste battery on calls or other things if you don't need them. Conserve your battery as much as possible. Consider buying an extra battery for emergency situations.

    Cell phone towers are unreliable though, so even if you have power you may not have service for days, since during a disaster, the government may not make fixing the cell towers a higher priority than getting food, water, shelter, etc. to the people.

- **Landline** – Some landlines do still work even if the power is out depending on the type of phone you have. It's worth looking into to see what kind you have. Many of us don't even have a landline anymore. In emergency situations a landline will still make outgoing calls if it's the really old kind that has the copper wire that feeds into the ground. If you have a newer home with updated phone jacks, your landline will probably be dead if the power goes out.

- **Phone Booths** – This is an extremely less traditional method, but it will work if you are out of other options. There are phone booths around, especially in bigger cities, and they are still very operational. It's worth doing a little research now to learn where the phone booths are in your city so if and when you need to use one, you know where the closest one is to you. Almost all phone booths are wired with the traditional copper wiring, which means they will still be operational if the power goes out. Cities have kept them this way for natural disasters and emergencies.

- **Satellite Phones** – This is another less traditional method, but nonetheless a method you could use in the event of a disaster. Most households do not have a satellite phone already, but you could purchase one to have in case there is a disaster. Satellite phones are reliable in as long as there are not problems with the satellites. So you don't need a tower like a cell phone, but you do need a satellite. A typical natural disaster like situation would not affect your ability to use a satellite phone. However, a terrorist strike or nuclear disaster could.

The other problem with a satellite phone is that they are costly. Not only is the phone itself pretty expensive, you also have to pay for a month subscription (like a phone plan), and minutes (also like a phone plan), in order to keep the phone operational at all times.

Chapter 3 – Use Technology

There are a lot of possibilities to use the technology that has been developed over the years to communicate with family and loved ones. In the event that we have access to our smartphones and the Internet or our cell phone plans, we can use that technology to easily communicate with each other even if we can't reach them directly because phone lines are jammed and overloaded with people trying to reach each other. Here are a few other options.

- **Text Each Other –** We are the generation of texting each other anyway so why should the day of a disaster be any different. If we can't reach each other through the phone line for whatever reason, a text message should suffice. It's almost easier to send a quick text back and forth relaying the information about a meeting point. As long as the information is clear and direct, a text message should easily suffice. The great thing about a text is you can send a group text to everyone and get the word out quickly about a meeting location and time – especially if there is a change.

- **Send an Email –** Your phone many not get service, or it might die. But if you have charge on your computer or tablet you can send an email out to your loved ones and friends. An email can send the information you would have sent in a text or would have relayed in a phone call. The great thing about an email is that you can send it to multiple people at one time. This is another reason why having everyone's email address is important. You may find that you don't have everyone's saved in your computer or tablet and it's handy to have them all written down when you need them.

- **Social Media** – Social media is new development that has really taken off in the last few years, but shouldn't be discarded when it comes to communication with family and loved ones. Social media can work in a couple different capacities. First the phone lines may be tied up and overloaded with people trying to get in touch with others making it difficult to get calls through. Instead of trying to make a call or multiple calls to family members, sending out a message via social media can alert family members that you can't be reached by phone and instead to meet at a certain destination or to try at a different number. This is when that code comes in handy since you might be broadcasting sensitive information to lots of people.

Another important part of social media is letting people know that you're okay. There will be lots of people that live outside of the state or even the country that are concerned about you're well-being. Social media is a great way to let others know that you and your loved ones are safe and out of harms way. There might be people that want to reach out to you or contact you and with social media you can let them know the best way they can help you.

- **Go Solar** – One last piece of advice is to start researching some solar power charging devices. Several companies have recently developed different charging devices that are completely solar capable. The great thing about these devices is that you can have power to devices like your laptop, cell phone, tablet, etc., when the power is down. The downside is that you can only charge your devices during the daytime and when it is sunny. So if there is inclement weather, it's cloudy, or you run out of charge during the night, you are up the creek without a paddle.

The upside is that at least you have an option. It gives you something where you had nothing before. These devices are affordable and nice to keep around during emergency situations. In addition to having car chargers and other emergency supplies, having solar charging kits are worth the investment.

Chapter 4 – Various Kinds of Radios

Radios are a great way to keep in touch with each other when things go south. In the event of a catastrophe, having a set of radios or even multiple sets of radios can give you peace of mind that you will be able to communicate with each other and keep in touch with what is going on in the outside world as well.

There are various types of radios, each with advantages and disadvantages. Let's talk about each of the different types and why you want to look into each of them. After looking at all of them, you can pick which type(s) work best for you and your family in the event of an emergency.

Perhaps this is somewhat obvious, but with all these radios, if you are trying to communicate with your own loved ones, you must possess two of these radios. In some cases you'll need multiple radios in order to communicate with everyone, which can become expensive.

- **Family Service Radio (FRS)** – This radio is extremely common and uses the FM frequency band. It has no testing requirements and also doesn't require any licenses, both of which are big advantages. Radios are also very affordable making it easy to have a radio for every member of the family if necessary. You'll be able to find these kinds of radios at most sporting goods stores, online, etc.

-

The major disadvantage of these radios is their range. The most common range is one mile. Sometimes they can range a little further, but you'll pay a lot more money for that feature and it won't get you that much more distance. There is also the fact that there will be a lot of interference, because there are a small number of channels you can broadcast on and there will probably be a lot of people using this kind of radio.

But these radios can be great for your family once you are close together. They are great for keeping in touch and staying connected. They may not be the best way to get connected initially, but they are a great resource for keeping together during the crisis since cell phone service may be sketchy and unreliable.

- **General Mobile Radio Service (GMRS)** – the GMRS radio is a good option that is a step above the FRS radio, but not extremely complicated. It does require a license ($85 for five years), but you don't have to go through any testing to operate the radio. There are also twenty-three different channels to broadcast on giving you more flexibility than the FRS radio.

The range on most GMRS radios is 6-12 miles, so a little further than FRS radios. However they do share some channels with FRS radios. This can be both an advantage and disadvantage depending on how you view it. As with other radios, there is a fair amount of interference because of limited channels and other people using the same type of radio.

- **Multiple Use Radio Service (MURS)** – This is a third type of radio that is very similar to the FRS and GMRS radio with one slight exception. The MURS radio only has six channels that it can work with and there is no license or testing associated with it. These radios range somewhere between three and ten miles.

One of the great advantages of this radio is that it can send voice, but it can also send data, which is the exception of any other radio on this list. These radios are also pretty affordable and do well in forested areas.

- **CB Radio** – CB Radios are a little outdated, but they can be great during an emergency. There are no restrictions with CB radios and no testing required to use them. They aren't very big or heavy, however the SSB version does have a rather obtrusive antenna. There are typically two types – an AM version and a SSB version. The AM version has a range of up to four miles whereas the SSB version has a range of up to 40-40 miles depending on terrain.

The CB radio is very user friendly and relatively cheap ($50 for a AM version), slightly higher for the SSB version. The big disadvantage is the range on the AM version and the fact that both are easily susceptible to interference and background noises. Users also often complain about the antenna on the SSB version.

- **Ham Radio** – This is probably the most complicated radio on our list, but also the best. With a Ham radio, you can broadcast on both the FM and AM frequencies, which is a major plus. However, you need both a license to use a Ham radio and you have to go through a testing procedure. If you plan to use a Ham radio, plan to dedicate anywhere between 10-20 hours to studying before your test to familiarize yourself with the rules and FAA specs.

The HAM radio isn't an ordinary radio, and can give you the range up to 100+ miles when you have access to a repeater. This can be extremely handy if you are looking for people in your group and/or trying to communicate with each other when you're extremely far apart.

A Ham radio doesn't need to feel intimidating, but it does require the most work of all the radios on our list. The cost to buy a Ham radio isn't extensive (usually around $60), but then you'll need study materials and the license on top of that, so you'll end up paying around twice the initial cost when you're done. However, if you think that becoming a certified Ham operator is worth your time, the money shouldn't scare you away from this.

The Ham radio definitely gives you the best radio with the biggest range and reliability during an emergency to contact both family and emergency personnel. As a Ham operator, you'll learn the frequencies that emergency responders use to communicate and how you can contact someone if you or a loved one needed help. It also gives you access to frequencies for things like weather and road updates. You could stay up to date with all the things happening around your city and know when it was safe to return home – assuming you weren't already there.

Chapter 5 – Out of the Box Ideas

When the world is crazy and the power is dead, you just might need a few ideas that are outside the box. These are definitely ideas that you will need to have discussed with family and loved ones beforehand or they will never think to look for them. They will be your last resort, but they just might come in handy when nothing else is working for you.

- **Fire/Smoke Signals** – Depending on the gravity of the situation, sending out smoke signals is a great option to communicate with your group. Often smoke is rising in various locations anyway from devastation through out the city and your smoke signals can be blended into the rest of the smoke. This is both a good thing and a bad thing. If your group is keen enough to recognize the smoke signals, they will easily be able to find you. However if they aren't, they might not recognize the smoke signals from the rest of the burning buildings.

So as long as you talk extensively and maybe even practice the smoke signals ahead of time, your group should be fine. You can even practice changing the color of your smoke depending on what things you choose to burn. The only caution we would give with this is that you may not always have certain things readily available. If you are afraid about the fire getting out of control, consider using a grill or something similar to keep the fire contained.

Fire and smoke signals don't only have to be used to get your group together either. You can continue using them to signal to your group once the group has been reunited. It's easy to send out a smoke signal that it's safe to bring back the food or that the building is all clear for them to enter.

- **Reflective Surfaces** – You can get really creative with this one, but think like mirrors, CDs, even women's make-up, etc. As long as you have access to the sun and can get the right angle, you can send light signals in various directions to people. This one can get a little tricky if you don't know which direction your group is traveling to or from. You can also become tired very quickly if you are trying to find them and aren't sure where they are. The biggest downside to this method is that it is ineffective during the nighttime.

However, once you are together, this is a great method to continue to communicate with each other about safety. This can be especially effective when you aren't sure whom else might be in your area and you want to make sure you are communicating with only your group. Think of it as a secret password.

- **Various Noises** – Again, like we've talked about before, these may seem completely out of the box, but when you're getting desperate, they just might come in handy. Think about things like air horns or bird calls that you as a group decide on beforehand. If you pick the noise and all agree that it is your noise, your family and loved ones will be drawn to it when they hear it.

It really doesn't matter if it is drums, whistles or duck quacks. What matters is that you all decided that it was your noise. When choosing a noise for your group, there are a few things to keep in mind. Some noises will travel farther than others, so you'll want to consider how far you want the noise to travel and whether you are worried about that specific factor.

You'll also want to consider whether or not you want your noise to blend in with your surroundings at all. Again, blending noises can be both a good and bad thing. Your family members could miss the noise, but so could others, which means attention won't be drawn to you.

An air horn, for example will definitely draw attention to you no matter what the situation. However bird calls, generally won't draw as much attention. So as long as your family and loved ones are listening for the sound and will follow it, you are safe to use something like a bird call and won't draw much attention both to you and your family members.

- **Flares** – Flares are a great way to alert family members to your location. A big downside is that they are also a great way to alert everyone else to your location also. So if you do resort to using a flare or flare gun, be prepared for company other than just your family. The company that comes may be friendly and just in need of some support, but it may also be unfriendly and looking to loot and pillage.

Flare guns can be used as a defensive weapon, but they aren't extremely effective especially depending what you're going up against. Flare guns are easy to purchase and don't require any background checks or licenses, so you don't need to worry about that. You'll be able to purchase them online or many places around many towns.

Most flares will burn for anywhere between half a minute to a minute. They can also be used anytime of the day or night and will burn bright enough to be seen by members of your family or other loved ones. Of course they are more effective at night, but if you absolutely needed to you could use one during the day also.

A word of caution though – flares are extremely hard to extinguish once lit, so don't waste them and make sure you really want one lit from the beginning. It can also be dangerous trying to extinguish one or getting it relit, so be careful.

- **Markers** – Think about ways you can signal for your group where you are headed and in what direction. We used to do this all the time when we were hiking in large groups. If one section of the group wanted to hike faster than the other, a leader would take the faster group and hike ahead. The slower group would hike behind with a second leader. If there was a fork in the path, the first leader would always leave some sort of marker to let the group in the back know which way the group in the front had travelled. That way the whole group never split.

- Sometimes it was a rock formation or sticks set into an arrow. The leaders always knew beforehand what to look for, but more importantly, they always knew to look for something.

- The great thing about using markers is that they can usually blend into their surroundings or can also be coded so others can distinguish them. For example if you use the code your family set up earlier, you can write something about a location or a time and only you and your group know what it means. That way those who would do your group harm or try and loot from you, can't find your location or don't know what time your party will meet together.

- If you choose to use things in the area, such as rocks, sticks, stones, etc. they often are walked right past without a second glance by most people.

22

They could also be mistaken for a child's creation rather than a signal or a marker indicating something important. For that reason, you do have to be somewhat cautious in leaving them, because people will knock them over, kick them out of the way, or simply be careless about them thinking they don't mean anything important. It's not that they are intentionally trying to destroy your marker; they just don't realize its importance.

- For that reason, it is safer to place your markers a little out of the way of most foot traffic. They still should be within normal eye of sight, so your party will see them, but enough out of the way so the rest of the world will leave them alone. Additionally, place enough markers along your path so if one is lost or destroyed your family can pick up the trail again a little further down.

- Another great alternative to the kind of markers we talked about is chalk. Many groups have and will continue to us chalk. Chalk is great because you can leave a mark, signal, code, etc. virtually anywhere for your family or group to recognize and know what to do. Chalk is hard to destroy if it is out of the way unless it gets wet. Chalk is also lightweight making it easy to carry if you are on foot. That way you don't have to worry about collecting objects to make your own markers for your group to find and worry about them missing a marker because it blends in with surroundings.

- Ultimately markers are a great way to connect with your group and signal directions, meeting places, times, etc. Just make sure you've communicated about them beforehand during your plan to ensure that your group is looking for them and remembers your code.

- **Bulletin Boards** – These are very old fashioned, but when the power is out and you don't have the traditional methods of communication, old fashioned is the way to go. One of the first things to think about is where the bulletin boards exist in town right now. If you're thinking about it, you'll probably have some at the library, recreation center, city buildings, etc. Maybe even keep track of them the next few times you go around on some of your errands, so you know where five to ten boards are in different locations.

- If you can't find or get in touch with family right away through phones, texting or email, bulletin boards might be a great way to leave a note for them. If they know to check certain boards because you've planned that early on, you can communicate that way. Leave them a note about a location where you will be next or where they can find you especially if you had to change locations or meeting places.

- Bulletin boards probably wouldn't be the first thing you thought of when you initially thought about locating each other, but when things get desperate, and they might, you'd sure be grateful you had things as a back-up plan in your arsenal of communication tools.

Conclusion

We all need to be prepared for the future and what it might bring. It doesn't matter if that future happens tomorrow or five years from now. We can all sleep better tonight knowing that we are prepared for whatever the future might bring. A major concern is the ability to keep in touch, stay together, and communicate with each other when everything breaks and using a few, some or all of the ideas in this book will give you the peace of mind that you can and you will be able to stay together when the future becomes unstable.

The communication tips in this book are designed to help you feel better prepared for the future and for the disasters ahead. They should give you the knowledge and the ability to look forward not from a position of fear, but from a position of strength.

We don't know what the futures holds for us, but when disaster comes, we will be prepared for it. Takes the steps now getting yourself and your family prepared by making a plan, communicating that plan and getting the equipment you need.

Made in the USA
Monee, IL
02 December 2020

50536871R00015